Crane Prairie
Deschutes Headwaters

Crane Prairie
Deschutes Headwaters

Scott Richmond

Frank Amato
PORTLAND

Volume 5, Number 4

◆

Acknowledgments

Jim Dexter, Fred Foisset, and Greg Price for flies, advice, and review of text. From the Confederated Tribes of the Warm Springs Reservation: Wilson Wewa of the Culture and History department for an overview of Indian use of the Crane Prairie area. From the US Forest Service: Larry Chitwood for a geologic history of the region. From the Oregon Department of Fish and Wildlife: Ted Fies for fish management and biology information; Corey Heath for insights into the birds of Crane Prairie; Terry Schrader for sharing results of the bass predation study. From the Colorado State University Department of Fishery and Wildlife Biology: Eric Bergersen and George Schisler for information on the survival of trout caught and released on scented artificial bait. The Deschutes County Historical Society for the early history of the Crane Prairie country.

Series Editor: Frank Amato
Kim Koch

Photography: Scott Richmond (unless otherwise noted)
Fly plates photographed by: Jim Schollmeyer
Design: Amy Tomlinson
Map: Amy Tomlinson

Softbound ISBN: 1-57188-095-X; Hardbound ISBN: 1-57188-096-8
(Hardbound edition limited to 350-500 copies)

© 1999 Frank Amato Publications, Inc.
P.O. Box 82112, Portland, Oregon 97282
(503) 653-8108
Printed in Hong Kong
1 3 5 7 9 10 8 6 4 2

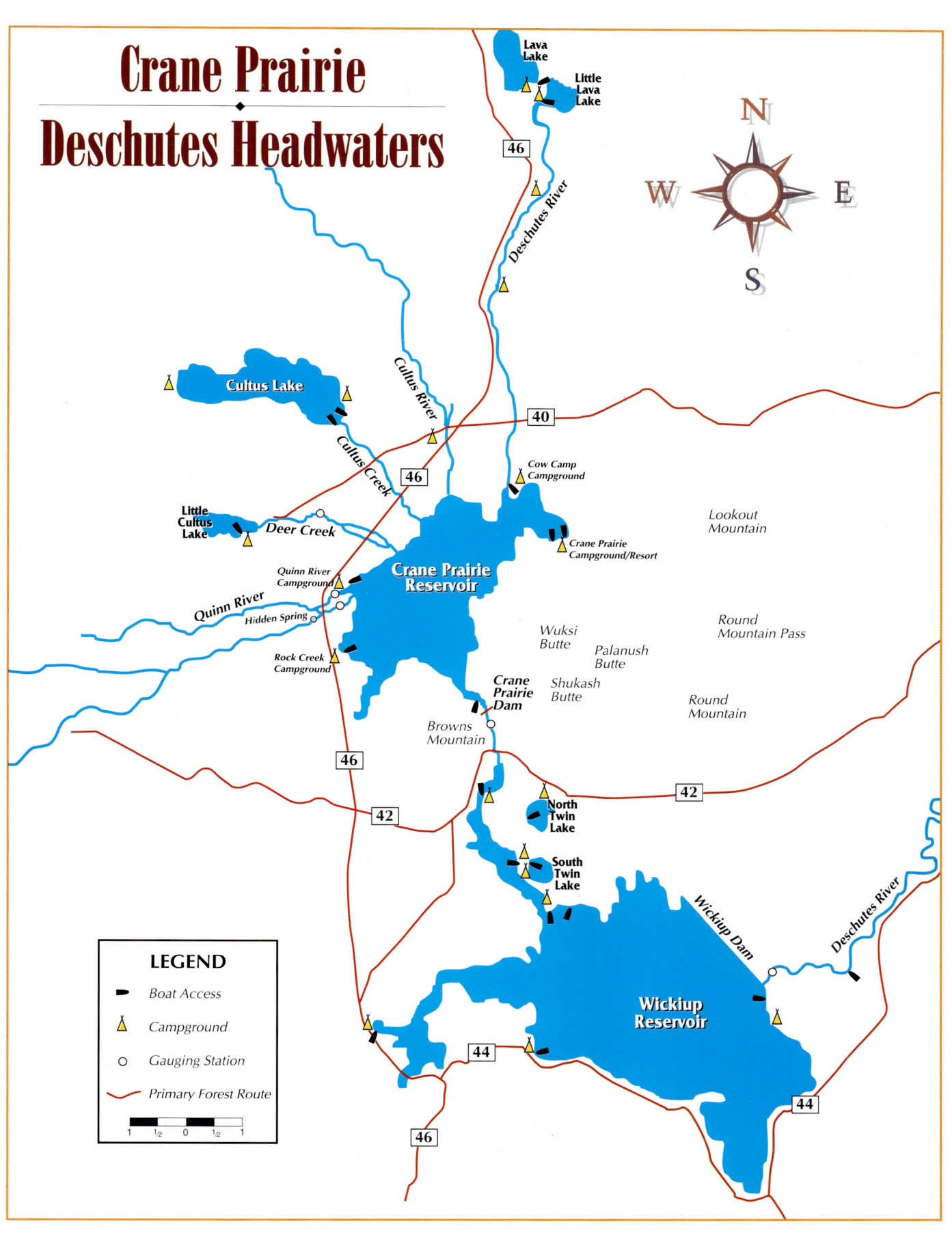

Fish on! Crane Prairie's rainbows are famous for long, fast runs.

Crane Prairie
Deschutes Headwaters

History

The small river wanders through the meadow like it can't make up its mind which way it wants to go. Blue-bodied damselflies rest among the wildflowers that grow on the riverbank. Scores of newly-emerged mayflies float briefly on the river's surface before flying off in search of a mate. Not all of them make the transition from river to sky, though. Fish—rainbow trout, Dolly Varden, whitefish, steelhead and salmon not yet gone to sea—compete for the mayflies, and many duns disappear in a swirl of water.

Although the fish are feeding eagerly, they are always alert for predators. Osprey, eagles, otters, and bear have taken a toll on their kin. So when a new creature appears, one never before seen by these fish or their ancestors, they move away from its shadow.

This new predator walks on two legs, legs which have carried him and his companions many miles. Animal trails are the only by-ways in this land, and legs the only transport. It will be twenty-five millennia before horses arrive on the continent, and four centuries after that before the automobile whizzes onto the scene.

Flies large and small and in-between will entice Crane's big rainbows.

The predator notes the presence of the trout; they will provide food when other quarry are not available. Suddenly his eyes narrow as he catches a movement on the other side of the meadow. He sees a slow-walking form, a giant sloth almost as large as the woolly, tusked beasts he and his band have hunted before. He grips his spear tighter and motions to his companions. This looks like a good place.

A young boy of ten summers plays alone near the river. Since his ancestors first came to this country, his people have gathered food, fished, and hunted here. It has been an active land, one that has changed radically and violently many times. The boy knows the stories, how they—the "new people"—were brought here, how they once travelled north to find a wall of ice, how today, though, the earth is quiet, and he hears the cry of an osprey high above him.

Birds are not the only animals using the meadow and its rivers. Signs of deer, elk, and other game are everywhere, and at his feet fish rest in the crystalline river, quietly finning under the bright summer sun. The boy crawls to the edge of the river and peers into it. Trout swim near the bank, and he slowly moves both hands into the water, then waits. Pursuing a drifting mayfly, a trout sidles near, and before it can escape, the boy has it in his quick hands. He puts it on the bank with two others. He plans to bring them home to his family for a meal. They will make a pleasant change from the usual fare of roots and berries. Truth be known, however, he enjoys catching the trout as much as eating them.

Captain John Fremont's party has established its camp, and the horses are led to the river to drink from its cool waters. The year is 1843, and Fremont has traveled north from California. He sits in his tent and makes a note in his diary: "Today we had good traveling ground, the trail leading sometimes over rather sandy soils in the pine forest, and sometimes over meadow-land along the stream. The great beauty of the country in summer constantly suggested itself to our imaginations; and even now we found it beautiful, as we rode along these meadows, from half a mile to two miles wide."

A man travels to a river-laced meadow his fellow homesteaders are calling Crane Prairie. His plan is to catch enough trout to help feed his family through the winter. His two sons join him after he's been fishing in the Deschutes River for a single day. They find that he has already filled a 50-gallon barrel with fillets, not one of which is less than 16 inches long. There seems to be no end to the numbers of big fish, and Oregon's catch limit, 125 trout per day, reflects that perception.

Herbert Hoover, 31st president of the United States, types the date—August 25, 1936—at the top of the letter he is preparing. Four years earlier, Franklin Roosevelt had bested him in a bitter campaign, and now Hoover is retired—at least temporarily—from public life. This gives him the freedom to return to Oregon, where he spent much of his boyhood. Fly fishing is his main recreation, and the pursuit of fish is the motive of today's letter. "If you would care to build a two room log cabin on your location, I would be glad to advance you the $200 to do so . ." he begins. The cabin is to be a base for fly fishing expeditions. Its site is a lake, but a river lies a scant 200 yards to the west. The river is rich, a fine place to fish, and many other excellent waters, both rivers and lakes, are scattered about this country. Maybe it's not so bad, not being president anymore.

An eleven-year-old girl casts a fly line. Her right arm moves in a steady rhythm and pauses at just the right moments. Her father has been a patient teacher, and she has learned well. "Good cast," he says, as the damselfly nymph makes a soft landing fifty feet away. They have come to this area every summer since the girl was a toddler, pitching the family tent at a campground in the lodgepole forest and enjoying the sunshine and scenery. Her father camped here with his parents when he was a youngster no older than she is now.

"Remember," he says to her, "Pull the line in slowly." She draws the slow-sinking line a few inches at a time, fighting the hurry-up feelings of youth. Ten feet of line comes in and piles on the floor of the boat in loose coils. She draws the fly in a few more inches, then feels a slight resistance. She tentatively moves the rod back a foot. Her line suddenly straightens and lifts from the water. The rod bends deeply with the pull of the big trout, the reel sings, and her father whoops, "Well done!" When the seven-pound rainbow trout is brought to the boat, she watches carefully as her father revives it. "Bye," she says as it is released and disappears into the green water. "See you later."

The Crane Prairie country has been a place of enjoyment, refreshment, and family pleasure for thousands of years. The Deschutes River has its modest beginning here. Its history in this headwater area is much different from that of the lower river. The lower Deschutes has spent a million years wearing a 1,200-foot-deep groove into ancient lava flows. But here, the earth has re-created itself in more recent times, and the upper river has often adapted to a changing landscape. Today, it meanders through gentle country and resembles a spring creek in a mountain meadow more than the big, brawling canyon-bound river of its lower reaches.

About 15,000 thousand years ago, the Crane Prairie country was a sediment-filled plain where rivers, creeks, and lakes dotted the landscape. It seems certain that humans had hunted and gathered food here. Then the earth cracked open, spilling lava over the plain and pushing the Deschutes River to

Float tubes can be used at Crane Prairie, but a boat gives access to more of the lake.

the west. The ground cooled and soil re-built, some blowing in from the south, some coming from glacial silt as the ice-age eased, and some falling from the sky when Mt. Mazama blew its top.

Grass, pine trees, and wildflowers rooted themselves in the soil, and a rich habitat for wildlife was created. The Deschutes River wandered through and was joined by several creeks and rivers. They provided a place for fish and other aquatic life, and once more the area became a prized gathering place for native peoples. In historical times, bands of Northern Paiutes camped here, using Crane Prairie as a base for hunting, root gathering . . . and fishing.

In the twentieth century, the landscape changed again, but this time it was man, not nature, that interrupted the course of the river. In 1922, a dam across the Deschutes flooded Crane Prairie. Although the dam was built to store water for irrigation, an unintended consequence was that it created one of the most productive stillwater trout fisheries in the U.S.

It should be remembered, however, that Crane Prairie teemed with big fish long before it became a lake. Furthermore, much of today's catch are wild trout directly descended from the original inhabitants. Rainbow trout and whitefish are the primary indigenous species still present. Stocked rainbows are added, but the majority of the catch is wild and spawns in the Deschutes between Crane Prairie and its source at Little Lava Lake. In addition to the rainbows, brook trout have been added from time to time. Although not native to the region, they reproduce naturally and most of them can be considered wild, if not native.

After leaving Crane Prairie, the Deschutes is free-flowing for four miles, then enters Wickiup Reservoir, another impoundment created by a dam on the Deschutes. Brown trout and landlocked coho salmon are present in this lake. Like Crane Prairie's brook trout, Wickiup's browns are not native, but natural reproduction is common and most fish qualify as wild. And big! Ten- to fifteen-pound browns are present in good numbers, and even bigger fish swim in the lake.

From Wickiup, to Crane Prairie, to the modest beginnings of the Deschutes, this region has provided a rich habitat for wild fish for millennia. Man is a recent arrival who has enjoyed himself here for countless generations. If we take care of it and teach the anglers of the future to do the same, Crane Prairie and the headwaters of the Deschutes will delight people for many more generations.

Fish

Why does Crane Prairie grow such large fish? The answer lies in the situation and structure of the lake. First, it is in a sunny place; the east slope of the Cascades is high and mountainous but still gets abundant sunshine for much of the year, making for a long growing season. Second, the lake is shallow, so the sunlight that falls on it penetrates the entire lake and stimulates plant growth everywhere. However, Crane Prairie would be poor trout habitat if not for the third factor: substantial inflows of cool water from several sources. Without the input of cold water (some from rivers and creeks, some from

Most fly anglers release all the trout they catch here.

springs) Crane Prairie's shallow depth would make the lake too hot to support trout. Fourth, the lake has a high pH, a factor known to encourage aquatic growth. Last, the snags and downed timber left in the lake create habitat for aquatic insects and hiding places for fish.

Crane Prairie supports trophy-sized game fish of several species: rainbow trout, brook trout, mountain whitefish, and largemouth bass. These species and other fish dwelling in the lake are described below.

Rainbow Trout

Rainbows are the primary target of Crane Prairie's fly anglers. Although the Oregon Department of Fish and Wildlife (ODFW) stocks 200,000 five-inch fingerlings a year, more than 50% of the catch comes from naturally spawning fish. Thus, many of the rainbows anglers catch here are wild trout. Most of these spawn in the Deschutes River above Crane Prairie, and ODFW has counted over 600 redds in the eight-mile stretch of river. Fortunately, this water is closed in the spring and fall to protect spawning trout.

The lineage of the wild rainbows is not certain. No doubt some are descended from hatchery stock, but there were native rainbows in this part of the Deschutes before Crane Prairie Dam was built. Therefore it is likely that many of today's trout carry the ancient genes that were native to the area.

The wild fish survive well, are more wary than hatchery fish, and seem to do better in low-water years. There has even been some talk of using them to replace some of the brood stock at ODFW's Oak Springs hatchery, a facility that raises most of the trout that the state stocks east of the Cascades. Regardless of their origin, all rainbows grow big and fat in a short time on Crane Prairie's abundant forage. Fish of five pounds are commonplace. Many are at least seven pounds, and some are even bigger. While trout over ten pounds have not been uncommon in the past, recently the average size has declined so that fish over seven pounds are rare. The reason for the smaller fish is not clear. It may be an effect of the drought years (from 1987 to 1994, only one year approached normal rainfall in Oregon), changes in the food supply due to overharvest of dragonfly nymphs or competition from bass, or other factors not well understood. However, even if the size of the trout has declined some, there are still many fish—both wild and stocked—in the five- to seven-pound class. And that's good news on any stillwater.

Crane Prairie's rainbows are bright fish with just a hint of pink on their flanks. Occasionally you will hook a skinny one, but most are deep-bellied and football-shaped, especially in the fall. While anglers best remember the big fish, the majority of the catch is 18 to 21 inches. Some jaded anglers refer to these trout as "mediocre," but the fact is that many of them put up a better scrap than their older siblings.

Brook Trout

Rainbows get most of the attention at Crane Prairie, but the lake also grows some very big brook trout. Obviously the brook trout are not indigenous to the area; however almost all of them qualify as "wild." They reproduce naturally in the lake and its tributaries, and the Oregon Department of Fish and Wildlife (ODFW) rarely stocks them. They are harder to catch than the rainbows, but some fly anglers actually target the brookies. I can't blame them. They're beautiful fish, especially in the fall, and it's not every lake that grows three- to five-pound brook trout.

Largemouth Bass

Bass are another non-native fish found in Crane Prairie. Unfortunately, these bass resulted from an illegal planting done sometime in the 1980s by unnamed pond scum. Like all other fish in this productive water, the largemouth grow big but, as with all fish in Crane Prairie, their size has gone down in recent years.

Formerly, a large population of tui chub (roach) lived in the lake, but water draw-downs devastated the chub, which favor shallow spawning grounds. When the chub were plentiful, the bass fed heavily on them and grew large—five-pounders were readily available. Since the decline of the chub, the bass feed primarily on insects, mostly damselfly nymphs, and there is no doubt that they compete with trout for food. In addition to insects, the bass eat frogs and snails and a few rainbow trout fingerlings.

This latter item is one of several reasons ODFW has taken a lot of heat from trout anglers over the bass in Crane Prairie. Many anglers believe the bass feed heavily on trout. ODFW has conducted studies of bass habits in the lake and has concluded they are not taking many trout. An exception was when hatchery fingerlings were released into the lake one spring near the resort. Because the water is shallow there, it is one of the first places to warm in the spring and becomes a congregating place for bass. When the hatchery truck dumped its contents, the bass thought it must be Christmas. They ripped through the fingerlings like hogs in fresh corn. Since then, ODFW has modified their stocking program to avoid this area. Analysis of bass stomach contents throughout the rest of the lake shows very few trout.

It's possible that the trout have received some small benefit from the bass. Because bass are surface-oriented, slow, highly visible, and inhabitants of shallow areas, Crane Prairie's osprey are quite fond of them. The osprey may actually prefer largemouth because they are easier to catch. And if trout have turned up in bass stomachs, not a few bass have been found inside large trout.

Other Species

Mountain whitefish are available in Crane Prairie. In fact, the Oregon state record whitefish came from here (is there no end to the large fish this lake can grow?). The whitefish are indigenous and self-propagating. They are seldom caught on fly tackle.

Kokanee are stocked in the lake, though during high-water years they propagate naturally in the tributaries. In spring and summer, kokanee concentrate in the Quinn and Cultus channels because they have little tolerance for warm water. Most are caught early in the season by trollers, and it is rare for a fly angler to hook one.

As mentioned before, tui chub are present. Although their numbers are greatly reduced from prior years, they are prolific little buggers and a couple of rainy years could cause the population to soar.

Another exotic (and undesirable) species is the three-spined stickleback, a common aquarium fish that has somehow found its way into Crane Prairie and other nearby waters. They serve as forage for bigger fish.

And recently a Crane Prairie angler caught a bluegill that shouldn't have been there. Sigh.

Tackle

Rods

Crane Prairie's trout are hefty, and there are lots of weeds and snags around which they can wrap your leader. In addition the wind can be strong enough to blow your breath back down your throat. For these reasons, I never venture onto this lake with anything less than a strong six-weight rod. There are days when a five-weight might work, and sometimes I've wished for a seven, but 90% of the time a good graphite six-weight is the right rod for the job.

Lines

When fishing Crane Prairie, I rarely use any lines other than a double-taper floater and an intermediate, usually a Wet Cel I. The intermediate is the line of choice for 75% of my fishing here. Most of the time you want your fly moving slowly just over the weed tops, and an intermediate line is the best way to do that. Occasionally I'll use a Wet Cel II, but usually I'd have accomplished the same thing with an intermediate and a little more patience. Some anglers favor the Scientific Anglers Mastery Stillwater line. It sinks faster than a standard intermediate, which will get you down too fast in some parts of the lake. However, its merits may outweigh its drawbacks.

A floating line has some use when fishing *Callibaetis* duns, stillborns, or (rarely) spinners. Also, it is sometimes effective during midge or caddis hatches. Usually, however, the best tactic for an angler after larger trout is a nymph or pupa fished a little deeper, and the intermediate line is the right tool.

Companionable fishing near Rock Creek.

Leaders

Proper leader selection is the most important decision a fly fisher can make on Crane Prairie. You're more likely to get away with a poor fly choice than a poor leader choice.

Because the water is usually clear and shallow, and because the fish see a lot of anglers, it is critical to separate the fly from the line as far as possible. Therefore, leaders need to be at least 12 feet long, and 15 feet is better. An 18-foot leader is even more effective, but not all fly anglers can handle it well, especially if the wind is blowing. Better a clean 15-foot leader than an 18-footer that looks like a Boy Scout was practicing knots on it. Crane Prairie's pros will even go to a 25-foot leader if it's a flat, windless day.

Tippet size is a tricky choice. Fly size will dictate part of this decision, but you have to decide how many fish you want to hook and how many you want to lose. When the lake heats up in summer it's better to use a heavier tippet so you can play your fish quickly and let them go without harm. I usually use a 3X tippet, or even 2X if the lake is murky. If I'm into a pod of smaller trout taking surface flies (or I'm feeling unusually frustrated or abnormally cocky), I'll go to 5X, but that's the exception.

Hatches and Other Food

Damselflies

Take a close look at Crane Prairie's standing snags in August. You'll find them thick with the shucks of damselfly nymphs. The lake is rich in these slender aquatic insects, and from May through July they are the meat and potatoes of every big trout's diet. The nymphs are active at the beginning of the season, but the July migration is peak time. Hoards of them converge on standing snags, crawl up above the water line, and emerge in the open air. After the migration and emergence, adult females return to lay eggs and are sometimes pulled under by eager trout.

Crane Prairie is rich damselfly habitat, but populations go through boom-and-bust cycles.

From Opening Day through July, damsel nymphs should be part of every angler's arsenal. The best patterns are slender and sparse.

Midges

Why would a seven-pound trout take a size 20 insect, even if bigger fare are available? The reasons may not be obvious, but it's clear that big rainbows like midges. The pupae are easy to get, and there's lots of them. Therefore, midges can be extremely important on Crane Prairie, especially in late summer and early fall. Fly patterns from size 16 through 22 are useful, in colors of black, gray, tan, and olive. Jim Dexter, a master fly tier who operates a fly shop in La Pine, showed me how to tie the most effective midge pattern I've ever used. Jim takes a peacock herl and strips the herl off. This leaves a gray-olive stem that is wound around the hook to make the body. Wrap it with copper wire, dub a small thorax with a dab of white ostrich herl sticking forward (for gills), and tie in tiny grizzly hackle tips downwing style.

Callibaetis

In past years, Crane's *Callibaetis* hatches were legendary. During a massive hatch, when 5- to 10-pound rainbows were sipping duns everywhere you looked, you'd swear you heard a dull thumping sound all over the lake; it was the pounding hearts of many anglers.

Recently, however, the *Callibaetis* hatches have been few and far between. It's not clear why they have declined. It may be a drought effect, or due to water drawdowns, or perhaps just a natural cycle that will eventually swing back to what anglers had come to feel was normal.

But decline doesn't mean extinction, and *Callibaetis* can still be important on Crane Prairie. The nymphs live in the weeds, which means you can find them anywhere in the lake. They hatch from May through September, but not with clockwork regularity. Fly anglers should always be prepared, however. The early season duns are about size 14, and they get smaller and darker as the season progresses.

Caddis

Crane Prairie has several kinds of caddis, and trout definitely can be selective on them, especially the rising pupae. Some species are fond of lounging on the surface, looking like crackers and cheese on a platter—and often meeting a similar fate in the mouth of a trout. While adult caddis are taken, the main story is subsurface where fish feed on rising pupae.

Hatches of the lake's caddisflies are often ignored by fly anglers — but not by trout.

CRANE PRAIRIE

Dragonflies are common at Crane Prairie. The larvae often provide a meal for trout.

Dragonflies
There was a time when Crane Prairie abounded in dragonflies. Their big nymphs could be found under any submerged log, and trout grew fat on them. Soon, though, another predator showed up and began taking the nymphs. This one was two-legged and plopped the big ugly critters into bait boxes and called them "hellgrammites." Now it's tough to find dragonfly nymphs at Crane Prairie.

Even though the fish are not as focused on them as they once were, a nymph pattern can still produce fish. Since dragonflies spend three years in the aquatic stage, they are available for a long time. Use a pattern of the thinner variety.

Leeches
It's hard to find a lake without leeches, and Crane Prairie is no exception. Leeches are a type of nocturnal aquatic worm that feeds on dead things. Like most North American leeches, Crane Prairie's species do not suck blood. The population has declined a bit in recent years, possibly due to largemouth bass. Good leech patterns can still entice fish, however, especially when used near dawn and dusk.

Flies
The fly plates on pages 46 and 47 show a variety of productive patterns for Crane Prairie. All can be effective, and some of them are indispensable under certain conditions. However, there are six that I would never venture onto the lake without. They are:

Black Leech, size 8
Olive Woolly Bugger, size 10
Brown Woolly Bugger, size 10
Gray-olive Midge Pupa, size 18
Flashback Pheasant Tail, size 16

And a good damselfly nymph pattern. What's good? Every year it seems to take a slightly different fly to entice the trout. Crane Prairie anglers probably expend more energy on developing new damselfly patterns than on any other activity.

Finding Fish
In pre-dam days, Crane Prairie was a flat expanse where stands of pines often gave way to open meadows. The Deschutes River entered from the north, but it was more like a creek than a river. Cold, and only ten or fifteen feet across, it was mostly shallow and ran fast. Every so often, though, the river-to-be slowed and deepened. Shallow riffles sometimes ended in pockets five or six feet deep and maybe 20 feet long. On the outside of the river's bends, deep slots often formed.

The Deschutes was not the only water running through the old Crane Prairie. Other streams—Quinn River, Rock Creek, Cultus River, Deer Creek—flowed into it. But each creek or river eventually joined the Deschutes and swelled its flow. The pretty creek that entered the prairie so modestly exited as a river of consequence.

When the floodgates of the dam were closed in 1922, the pines were left standing. A couple of times after that, the reservoir was drained enough to allow logging of some of the standing timber. The practice soon ceased, however, and anglers of later generations reaped the benefits.

Today, the old creek beds and flooded timber are two of the keys to finding Crane Prairie's big trout.

In early season, the water is at its highest level and most of the lake is fishable. The rivers that flow into Crane Prairie are bone-chilling cold with snow melt and spring water. Once the water reaches the lake, however, it has a chance to warm—if the nights and days aren't colder than the rivers. At this time of year, an angler will find the most reliable fishing when he seeks out water warm enough to make a cold-blooded trout think about eating. This will be at the south end of the lake and sometimes in shallower areas such as near the resort. As the lake warms to typical summer temperatures, trout will more likely be found in the old river and creek beds. Here the water is both cooler and deeper, and vestigial currents concentrate food. Water drawdowns for irrigation (usually a September and October phenomenon) can also force fish into the channels.

Therefore, through the summer months and into the fall, successful fishing in Crane Prairie usually means finding the old river channels, especially the deep pockets.

Master fly-tier Jim Dexter constantly invents new fly patterns for Crane Prairie.

CRANE PRAIRIE

South Sister is one of several volcanic peaks that dominate Crane Prairie's skyline.

The locations of the channels are well known and are marked on any map of the lake. Unfortunately, what seems so obvious and easy to find on an 8 1/2 by 11-inch map can be quite elusive when you're in a small boat trying to find a 15-foot-wide ribbon on 5 square miles of weed-covered lake bottom. It would be a lot easier if someone would paint the channels black so it would look more like what you see on the maps!

Until that day, however, anglers will spend much time trying to locate the channels. There are three simple ways to do this. One is to see where everyone else is fishing and sidle up next to them. Another is to patiently ping the bottom with a depth sounder. A third is to venture on the lake when the sun is high and the surface calm. Under these conditions, you can often find the deeper water if you move slowly and look carefully. Sometimes you can see how the depth changes underneath you, and under the right conditions you can detect enough color change in the water to identify a channel from a distance.

While the channels often promise the best fishing, Crane Prairie's big trout have definite preferences for where they lie within the channels. Remember how the pre-dam streams had deep pockets and slots? Those pockets and slots are still there, and that's where the big ones are more likely to hang out—the water is cooler, the protection is better, and food collects and settles there.

Locating these holes, which may only be 20 feet across and three feet deeper than what surrounds them, can be tricky work. Talk about trying to find a needle in a haystack! Even experienced Crane Prairie anglers can have a tough time re-locating a favorite midsummer spot.

Once you've located a channel (or better, a deep pocket), park your boat or float tube off to the side of it and two casts away from your nearest neighbor. The key is to be out of the channel so you can cast into it. That way you will not disturb the fish, and you leave more room for other anglers. Don't sit on top of the channel itself unless you enjoy going fishless while other anglers hurl epithets questioning your intelligence, parentage, and prospects of leaving the lake alive.

If you're in a boat and you want to catch the best of Crane Prairie's trout, approach the good water carefully. Shut off your outboard a hundred feet or more before you get to a desirable spot. Then carefully and quietly bring yourself into position with gently-handled oars or, better yet, an electric motor. Always make sure you are at least two casts away from the nearest anglers so you are not crowding their water. Once in position, lower your anchors slowly, and don't bang around in the boat. Stealth will win you more fish—and more friends.

Temperature is another major factor in finding fish. Even in summer, Crane Prairie can have significant temperature gradients. One August, I measured the water temperature at the south end at 68 degrees. A couple of miles away, nearer the Deschutes inlet, the water was ten degrees cooler. Not only was the temperature significantly different, but the cooler water was crystal clear while the south end looked like algae soup. These kinds of gradients can be exploited by knowledgeable anglers. For example, while 68-degree water is at the edge of the good-fishing temperature scale, the algae serves to hide your leader and can make trout a bit bolder.

Tactics
Retrieves And Presentations

As stated earlier, at Crane Prairie most flies should be presented on a slow-sinking intermediate line with a long leader (15 to 18 feet) tapered to 3X or 4X. When you are rigged like this, nothing works better than a slow retrieve. The line gradually sinks and the fly creeps past the weed tops. This is the prime feeding zone for Crane's big rainbows. Although they often are looking up and will rise to intercept a good-looking morsel, they prefer to take their food near the cover of the weeds.

Other than depth, the key element is speed, or lack thereof. Your fly should barely move; the slower the better. If it isn't so slow that it's driving you nuts, you're doing it wrong. If there is one thing that should be engraved in the brain of every Crane Prairie fly angler, it's this: *intermediate line, long leader, painfully slow retrieve.*

On some lakes trout are "gulpers" that cruise just under the surface and suck down insects as they travel. Books and magazines often advise fly anglers to "cast ahead of the fish."

The underwater and standing snags shown in the photos below are key reasons for the lake's productivity.

CRANE PRAIRIE

When you get to Crane Prairie, though, put the books and magazines away because that strategy rarely works here.

For one thing, these trout are not gulpers. I see this feeding behavior less than 5% of the time at Crane Prairie. The second thing is to realize that the fish are seldom going where you think they are. If you get a good enough look at a rising trout to tell which direction it is swimming, then cast ahead of it to where you think it will be (as the books recommend), you will go fishless. That trout probably was sitting near the bottom, then came up through five feet of water to an insect four feet to either side of its lie. But after inhaling its meal, it went back to its lie. If you had cast ahead of where that fish rose, your fly will be eight or ten feet from where the trout is lying. The trout's momentum carried it that direction, but the fish circled around and went back to its original lie rather than hang around the surface.

Why is this? Take a look at (and listen to) the air around Crane Prairie. This is the largest nesting site for osprey in the Pacific Northwest. They're everywhere, as are cormorants and eagles. Any fish that lounges near the surface waiting for its meal will soon become some bird's lunch.

Dealing With Wind

As you might expect, a lake this big offers little to impede the breeze, and Crane Prairie gets its share of wind and whitecaps. Under windy conditions, casting becomes a chore—sometimes a dangerous one—and maintaining a slow, steady retrieve is nigh impossible. In addition, small boats and float tubes can be at risk if they are in the wrong part of the lake. The biggest blows come from the south and west, so finding shelter near those shores is a good strategy when the wind kicks up. Under these conditions, the worst waves (and casting conditions) occur at the east end of the large open section of the lake. However, as you continue to move east the standing timber offers some shelter, and quieter conditions can be found near the east end of the lake along the Deschutes channel.

On the other hand, too little wind can be a problem, too. The light breezes come from the north and east and are usually accompanied by clear weather—and by poor fishing. When the sun is high and nothing riffles the water's surface, trout see your furred-and-feathered fraud with ultimate clarity and are reluctant to strike. It's not impossible to catch fish in these conditions, but it can be frustratingly difficult.

On a day of sunny skies and light and variable breezes, the best strategy is to seek water that has a slight wind riffle on it. I recall a fine September day when my float tube was one among many in the Rock Creek area. Rising fish—some of them large enough to make you hyperventilate—frequently broke the calm surface. The only disturbance on the water was the big bow waves the trout created as they gobbled another emerging midge. All the anglers in the area were casting to rising fish, but none was successful, including me. Feeding fish were obvious and tempting to all of us, but we were equally obvious and far less tempting to the fish. I looked behind me to see what I should have noticed an hour earlier: patches of wind-riffled water. No fish could be seen rising in

A typical Crane Prairie rainbow — big-shouldered and well-fed — rests in algae-thickened water before being released.

them, but I cast my pupa there regardless. On the third cast, the line tightened and I was soon releasing a fat six-pound rainbow. After that, I skipped the flat water with its rising trout and fished only the wind-riffled patches where my line and leader were less obvious.

Time Of Day

It's often said at Crane Prairie that all the big fish are caught between 10 a.m. and 5 p.m., with a brief bite near sunrise. There is enough truth to this that many accept it without question. However, it is important to understand both the reasons behind this truism and the exceptions to it.

When the sun first peeks over the ridgeline, a moderate breeze is created and the water turns from flat calm to riffled. As long as the breeze continues, the fishing can be excellent. On many days, however, this only lasts about half an hour, then the water goes flat calm until around 10:00 when the wind usually picks up again. This is the situation most summer days, when the lake has its highest fishing pressure. But if the day starts cloudy and breezy and stays that way—as it often does in spring and late fall—fish can start hitting at sunrise and keep going all day.

I have to admit, though, that I have rarely had good fishing for large trout after 5:00 p.m. And I have no idea why. It seems like the big trout go home to watch the evening news and turn the food over to the youngsters. You can have wonderful fishing for 10- to 15-inch rainbows in the evening, but big fish are rare.

The exception to this is near dark. In Oregon, you can legally fish up to one hour after sunset. At Crane Prairie it can be dark, and I mean black, half an hour after sunset. To those prepared—flashlight and warm clothes, full stomach, and empty bladder—this is an excellent time to tie on a leech pattern and work it through the channels and among the snags.

Callibaetis

At Crane Prairie, all stages of this insect can be important: nymph, hatching dun, dun, and spinner (both upright and spent). My personal feeling, however, is that the nymph and hatching dun stages are most valuable to fly fishers. Many anglers wait until the hatch starts before tying on a *Callibaetis* dun imitation, but this is a mistake. Trout focus on the nymphs well before the first dun lifts off the water. When the *Callibaetis* have been active, a Flashback Pheasant Tail or similar fly can be deadly. Fish it on an intermediate line beginning in early morning. It can produce right through the hatch and into afternoon and evening.

Another important stage is the hatching dun. Trout seem to recognize the profile of this stage and know the insect isn't going anywhere soon, so they focus on it more than on the duns, which could fly away at any time. This imitation is fished on a floating line with a chuck-and-sit presentation.

Sometimes, however, the hatch is on and nothing seems to work. I found this true one blustery day in May. Three of us were in a rental boat casting to the huge trout that were rolling all around us. Nothing worked—not nymphs, not dries, not hatching duns. We tried every fly in the box, every presentation in our arsenal. Fish ignored us like we were fools with no right to exist on their water. One of us gave up on the hatch and tied on a damsel nymph. Within ten minutes he was releasing a 26-inch rainbow. Sometimes, it is more effective to switch to a subsurface fly that imitates food that is present but not hatching. Since that day in May, I have talked to people who always cast a damsel pattern during Crane's *Callibaetis* hatches. I haven't gone that far, but I agree that sometimes it is a good strategy.

Crane Prairie's underwater snags provide habitat for a variety of aquatic insects.

Midges

Midge pupae are traditionally fished just subsurface on a floating line, but at Crane Prairie that tactic will probably yield smaller fish than other approaches. A better tactic is to string your rod with an intermediate line, then tie your pupa to a long leader (at least 15 feet) and retrieve slowly. This puts your fly deeper and will yield bigger trout than fishing near the surface.

Another tactic is to use a floating line and an indicator. Use a lightly-weighted pattern or put a small amount of lead on the leader. Cast out and let the rig sink toward the bottom. After a minute or so, retrieve slowly so the fly rises toward the surface. If there is no take, stop and let it sink, then retrieve again.

As on any lake, Crane's midge hatches can be the very devil to match. One day I couldn't buy a trout, even though big brookies and rainbows were feeding near the surface. I was convinced they were taking midges, but wasn't sure of the size. When I don't know what's going on (which I admit is often) I adopt a "Monte Carlo" strategy and play the odds: I tie on several flies at once, each one a different color and/or size. Then I let the trout tell me their preference. Sometimes it works, sometimes it just results in a hopelessly tangled mess of flies and leader. This day, I put a size 18 midge on a dropper and a size 20 on the point and retrieved it slowly near the surface. Soon a big wave pushed up near my fly and I tightened on a nice rainbow.

My biggest concern was to get the trout near enough to my boat to see which fly he took: the big one or the little one. As I ran my hand down the thin leader, the trout surged and broke off . . . and pain shot through my left forefinger. I looked carefully; the little fly was gone but the bigger fly was still there, impaled up to the bend in my finger. Thank you, God, for giving us barbless hooks! My finger may have hurt a bit, but I'd gotten the point (so to speak) about which fly to use.

Leeches

Leeches swim through jet propulsion, taking in water at one end and squirting it out the other. Under normal conditions they swim with a pulsating, up-and-down motion. When pursued, they turn on the afterburners and move pretty fast. These characteristics give the clues for tying successful patterns and presenting them to trout.

First, leeches are light-shy, so you will probably be most successful fishing a leech pattern near dawn and dusk. Second, use a pattern that is most heavily weighted in the head; this gives your fly the undulating motion of the natural critter. Third, retrieve in slow strips about two feet long, pausing slightly between strips.

I know some very good fly anglers who always fish a leech pattern with a fast retrieve. The theory is that their fly will look like a leech trying to escape, thus stimulating an aggressive response from a trout who sees it streaking past its nose. That works in some lakes, but I've never found it effective at Crane Prairie. A few anglers claim success here with a fast retrieve, but I can't think of a single decent fish I've hooked on Crane Prairie when I've stripped in line at anything but a slow pace.

Where are the trout today? Anglers plot their strategy.

Caddis

Sometimes I feel like an idiot, but probably not as often as I should. I was on the lake at mid-morning in early September, and trout were feeding near the surface. I'd picked up a few fish on a midge pupa earlier, but now my casts were disdained. Why? What had changed and why couldn't I figure it out?

These fish had been rising over an hour. Some of the rises were subsurface, some right on top, and every now and then a trout shot out of the water like a missile. *Callibaetis?* No duns graced the water's surface. Midges? Earlier, yes, but while many adults still buzzed across the water it didn't look like a midge hatch.

I looked past my boat's eight-horse outboard. A brown insect with very long antennae rested on its black surface. I knew it was a caddis; they'd been around all morning, but not in any numbers. Another one settled down on the motor. "Maybe you'd better look a bit closer," I said to myself (at the end of a three-day solo trip like this I always talk to myself, especially when the trout don't want my flies). Suddenly I realized the air was filled with caddis. Obviously they were hatching in large numbers and the trout were keyed on the pupa. Duh.

I rummaged through my fly box looking for a suitable pattern. It was the end of the season, and the box was depleted. The best I could come up with was a brown soft hackle, size 14. In my experience, trout feeding on caddis pupae in fast, freestone rivers generally take the pupae near the bottom or near the surface, but seldom in between. In lakes, however, the pupae are often taken on the rise. My plan was to cast my lightly-weighted soft hackle at the end of a floating line, let the fly sink, then retrieve line so as to raise the fly quickly to the surface. On my first cast, however, the fly never got more than a foot-and-a-half deep before the line zipped out and I was into a decent trout.

Crane Prairie hosts large numbers of stillwater caddis. They hatch irregularly, and when they do most anglers are caught flat-footed. The first thing is to recognize that a hatch is happening. The principal signs are: fish feeding at all levels, from subsurface to surface; trout coming clear out of the water as they pursue rising pupae; no adult insects on the surface, but many in the air.

Once you recognize a hatch, skip over your dry flies and pick a wet. A good Sparkle Pupa can work well, and in a pinch a soft hackle of an appropriate size and color will do. I prefer a lightly-weighted fly that will sink slowly. Many of the takes will occur on the way down. If you get no action on the drop, retrieve line so the fly raises toward the surface. Still no take? Let it sink again, and repeat the lift-and-settle retrieve until it's time to cast again.

Damselflies

As stated earlier, the best damselfly nymph patterns are sparse, and the best presentation of them is slow. Use an intermediate line and retrieve so your fly creeps just over the tops of the

South Sister and Rocky Point.

CRANE PRAIRIE

conditions, and some he ties just to satisfy his own whims. All are effective under the right conditions. But nymphs are not the only stage of damselfly life that Jim ties. "Once," he says, "I was in my float tube when I saw rising trout, big ones. They wouldn't take my nymphs, and that always bugs me, so I checked it out. I saw that all the rises were near snags, and nymphs were crawling up to emerge on them. The wind was blowing adults into the water before their wings dried. They were helpless on the water and the fish knew it. They ate them up like popcorn. I went home and tied up some adult patterns, but instead of a normal wing I tied in a loose pillar of white poly-yarn."

"Did it work?" I asked him.

He closed his eyes and shook his head like he was remembering a favorite girlfriend. "Eat 'em up, pup," he said. "The next day the trout almost climbed down my throat to get at that fly."

Old Reliable

Crane Prairie isn't all massive hatches and trout climbing down your throat, however. Some days—make that a lot of days—nothing much seems to be happening. The odd rise disturbs the surface, but there are few clues (or too many clues) as to what the fish are after. What do you do when you don't know what's happening? Or when nothing seems to be happening?

My favorite fallback fly for lakes—my Old Reliable—is a size 10 olive Woolly Bugger. It works everywhere, and Crane Prairie is no exception. Trout might take it for a damselfly, a dragonfly, or a leech. Or just something that looks alive and tasty. The point is, *it works.* Like all other wet flies on Crane Prairie, I tie this one onto a long leader behind an intermediate line and retrieve it very slowly. I like to carry two colors of the fly: a dark olive and a lighter yellow-olive.

Somewhere down there, there's a trout! The lake's experts pick their anchoring spots with great care.

weeds. How slow is slow? Jim Dexter tells a story about the July he was catching four or five big rainbows an hour. A fishless angler noted Jim's frequently doubled rod, compared it with his own perpetually straight one, and rowed over to find the reason for the difference. "He was real careful," Jim recalls. "He rowed quietly and came around the outside so he wouldn't disturb the fish. I like it when people are considerate like that." The fishless angler asked Jim what fly he was using, and Jim showed it to him, even offering him a sample to use.

"That's too skinny!" said the angler, refusing the fly. "What's your retrieve like?"

Jim showed him his retrieve, which was about the pace of a lame snail.

"That's too slow!" said the angler.

Jim shrugged and went back to catching big trout. The other angler returned to his place and resumed casting his too-fuzzy nymphs and retrieving them too fast. His rod stayed straight.

Jim is a master of Crane Prairie's damselflies. He ties over a dozen different nymph patterns. Some imitate a species that begins migrating two weeks before other species, some have slight variations in color for different water, weed, and sky

Access

Drive-in Access

All the roads around Crane Prairie are part of the Forest Service system. Primary roads have two digits (e.g. 46) and most are paved. A secondary road has four digits, the first two of which indicate which primary road it intersects (e.g., secondary road 4270 intersects primary road 42). Primary roads are usually paved, but most secondary roads are dirt or gravel. A spur road is identified with seven digits, where the first four show which secondary or primary road it intersects. Spur roads are of variable quality. Some are paved and lead to developed campgrounds, but many are dirt and barely passable; some are not passable at all in normal passenger cars.

Roads around Crane Prairie are shown on the map. Following are some additional notes on a few of the roads.

Road 4270 skirts the east side of the lake and is paved. A paved spur leads to the resort and Crane Prairie Campground. Several other spur roads lead west toward the lake from 4270, but only two (4270-200 and 4270-470) give access to the water. Both are single-lane dirt and quite rough.

Road 4270-200 starts two miles south of the resort turn-off and is unsigned; there is a place to launch small boats 0.8 miles

CRANE PRAIRIE

from 4270. The road continues past the launch (stay left at the fork), and there is a good float tube launching point at the end.

Road 4270-470 is about a half-mile long and begins 0.4 miles from the resort turn-off. It is also very rough, especially near the end.

Road 4285 is a four-mile gravel road around the south shore between roads 42 and 46. Many rough dirt spurs lead to the lake, but the majority are unsuitable for most vehicles.

Boat Launching
Boats may be launched at the following ramps:

Crane Prairie Campground. A double concrete ramp with dock is near the day-use area. The ramp on the right (as you face the water) is best under low-water conditions. There is a large parking lot suitable for vehicles with trailers.

There is also a single concrete ramp on the "blue" loop; it is not usable when the water is low. This ramp is used primarily by those camped nearby, and there is no parking.

Rock Creek Campground. There is a paved ramp, but it is not very useful after mid-July because the water is too shallow when the lake is low, and the area clogs up with weeds.

Quinn River Campground. A concrete ramp puts you into the Quinn River a few hundred yards from the lake. There is usually sufficient water to launch unless you have a very deep drift boat. Watch for sunken logs in the river, however.

Dam. There is a dirt launch near the dam off road 4285. Because it is near the dam, there is always enough water to launch. Parking is limited, however.

Some people launch small boats and canoes from road 4270-200; see page 24.

The Forest Service lists a launch at Cow Meadow Campground, but heaven knows why. It dumps you into the Deschutes above the lake and is unsuitable for motored craft. And if you float to the lake in a canoe, it's a long paddle back upstream.

Bank Fishing Access
Crane Prairie has over 12 miles of shoreline, about 283 feet of which is suitable for bank fishing. The few good places are listed below.

Rock Creek. Park at a turn-out on road 46, 0.6 miles north of the entry to Rock Creek Campground. There is a gate; park so you don't block it. A trail leads three-eighths of a mile to a rocky point.

Big Rock. Take road 4270-200. There is decent bank access on the big rock, but it is mostly used by bait fishers.

Road 4270-475. Take this road to the end and wade into the water. If the wind is at your back, the Deschutes channel is at the limit of your best cast.

Float Tube Access
On many lakes, I put my float tube in my boat, motor to where I want to fish, park the boat on shore and fish from the tube. That strategy doesn't work at Crane Prairie because of the lake's

Long casts can improve your chances because the distance reduces the likelihood of spooking fish.

structure. However, there are a few places suitable for tubing.

Rock Creek. The cove south of Rocky Point often has good fishing, especially in the Rock Creek Channel. Except in early season, don't launch at the campground's boat ramp; it's too weedy and shallow. Instead, carry your tube north along the shore until you get closer to the point. An alternative is to park on road 46 and walk to the point (see bank access section above).

Quinn River. You can launch here (see boat launching section on page 23) and kick out to the lake, but you will get a lot of exercise before you reach good fishing in the channel next to the trees.

Road 4270-475. The end of this road puts you near the Deschutes channel and in an area that often has good fishing. Be aware that the road is quite rough.

Resort. Few people do this, but in spring when the lake is full and the fish are scattered, the area in front of the resort sometimes has good fishing. Launch your tube from the day-use area and give it a try.

Boat Access

Most of the season, Crane Prairie is best fished from a boat. It's a big lake, and even when the fish are concentrated in the channels you can't reach them from shore, and it's too far to kick a float tube.

The snags and underwater structure are two factors that make Crane Prairie a great place to fish, but they also mean you need to be a cautious boater. Even in the middle of the lake, you can run into a broken log lurking just below the surface. Sometimes the only indication of a deadhead is a cormorant perched on it. The lake has a 10 mph speed limit (often violated, but it keeps the water skiers away), but sometimes it pays to go even slower unless you know the water extremely well.

Late in the season the water level can be quite low, and much of the lake is too shallow for boating.

Another hazard is wind. On water this big, wind can whip up some pretty good whitecaps. For this reason, Crane Prairie is not a very good lake for canoes. If you use a canoe always keep your weather eye peeled, and head for shore as soon as it starts to blow.

Deschutes River
Little Lava Lake To Crane Prairie

I parked my car behind the white Ford Explorer, and in front of the green, ten-year-old Chevy. Two more cars were parked on the other side of road 40; one was new and trendy, the other old and showing signs of rust. An even split, I figured, between new fly anglers and old bait fishermen.

I followed the trail upstream along Deschutes Creek. Actually, it's officially called a "river," but at this stage of its life it's only 15 feet wide and shallow, and I have trouble thinking of it as anything but a creek. The pines are not thick here, and grassy meadows and wildflowers thrive, especially near the water. A bird-shaped shadow glided past my feet, and I looked up to see an osprey just 20 feet overhead. A 12-inch rainbow hung from his talons.

The creek/river meandered through the pines and meadows, occasionally splitting around an island. Water like this invites a dry fly, and the first fly angler I passed was casting one upstream to promising water just below a small island. "Any joy?" I asked.

When Wickiup Reservoir is drawn down in the fall, it reveals one of the reasons for its productivity — large woody debris.

Above Crane Prairie, the Deschutes River is a small creek.

River Journal

He shook his head. "Just a few little ones."

I knew what he meant by "little ones," because a few casts of my Parachute Adams had already attracted three fish, none of them more than four inches long. All that could be said for them was that if they avoided osprey and anglers they might grow larger, and they kept you from having to admit to being skunked.

A mosquito landed on my left hand. I swatted it and noticed a red spot nearby; I'd gotten one pest, but another had already come and gone, taking blood and leaving a welt. I felt little feet crawling along my right ear and swatted it, then wiped the black mosquito remains on my jeans.

I came to a place where the Deschutes deepened into a slow, dark pool. On the other bank, a scowling woman in shorts sat near a tree. She smacked her leg with a hand, then ran her fingers across her face like she was brushing something away. A few feet from her, an angler was dispatching a fish with a rock. "How big?" I asked him.

He looked pleased as he held up a nice 15-inch brook trout.

Just above Wickiup Reservoir, the Deschutes River meanders through grassy meadows and provides good brown-trout fishing.

I didn't ask what he'd caught it on: I could see the worm canteen on the bank next to his spinning rod. "On the bottom?" I asked.

"Yup," he said. He looked at his fish. "Tomorrow's breakfast."

"Cook it yourself," said his female companion as she sprayed Off! on her forearms.

He shrugged and strung a fresh worm on his hook.

At its confluence with the Columbia River, the Deschutes River is huge. It is one of the biggest rivers in Oregon, and it flows into the biggest river in the West. But up here where it begins on the east slope of the Cascades, the Deschutes is a mere trickle leaking out of Little Lava Lake. It's not an auspicious beginning for what will become one of the West's most famous rivers. While Little Lava is in a pretty setting, it is a small lake, barely 100 acres, and is an undistinguished fishery. The only trout are hatchery plants, and the lake is so unproductive they never grow to any size.

As the Deschutes leaves Little Lava, springs and small creeks add to its flow, and by the time it arrives at Crane Prairie eight miles later you could grant that it might someday grow up to be a river.

It's a pretty little stream, flowing through pine-scattered meadows and nourishing wildflowers on its banks. Mostly shallow and narrow, it occasionally gathers into slow, deep pools. Unfortunately, it is poor fly water. Dredging a nymph or a streamer through these pools can produce decent fish, but you have to admit that the worm-drowners are going to be far more productive than the fly fishers.

Both brook trout and rainbows come up from Crane Prairie, but they are smaller than the fish you'll find in the lake. The exception is spring and fall, when rainbows and brooks, respectively, enter the stream to spawn. Fortunately, open season for this stretch of the Deschutes runs only from June 1 through August 31.

During the open season, access is easy since road 46 parallels the stream for most of its length. Trails follow both sides of the river. They are well-beaten paths: the area's scenic charms are obvious to everyone driving past, and it's rare not to see at least one car in every pullout. This is not an area for summer solitude.

The meadows make a pretty setting, though—one hard for fly anglers to resist. It looks like classic dry-fly water, like something you'd see in a movie or a magazine, and few fly anglers can resist casting themselves for a starring role here. Keep in mind, however, that those beautiful meadows host huge numbers of ravenous mosquitoes. Angler/actors should be prepared with repellent and canvas shirts, and keep one hand free for smacking the blood-thirsty pests. If you venture forth clad in T-shirt and shorts, you'll soon look like a victim in a grade-B vampire movie rather than the star of *A River Runs Through It*.

Deschutes River
Crane Prairie To Wickiup

An angler walks along the Deschutes River above Wickiup. Expectation quickens his stride. The sun is just kissing the western ridgeline, and he zips his jacket, knowing that in late August the evening air chills quickly even if the day is hot.

He slows as he comes to a bend in the river, then crouches and, almost on hands and knees, travels another 50 feet. Kneeling amid the tall grass, he keeps his rod low while he unhooks a large Matuka-style fly from its keeper. He casts carefully, knowing from experience just where on the opposite bank he should place the big streamer. The fly lands where he wants it. He counts to three as it drifts into the undercut, then he strips line. He moves it barely a foot before a heavy weight hits. His rod arcs deeply, and line rips from his reel like it is tied to a galloping horse.

Ten minutes later he holds his rod high behind him as he runs his hand down the leader to the big trout lying on its side in the river. He grasps its tail with his left hand; after laying down his rod, he unhooks the fly with his right hand. He slowly moves the trout back and forth. The post-sunset light is poor, but he can still make out the yellow-brown belly, the big orange spots, the massive jaws. "Big male," he says to himself. "Twenty-three, maybe twenty-five inches. Five pounds, easy."

The brown trout pulls once on his hand, but he hangs on. One more pull, and he lets it go into the dark water.

When the Deschutes escapes from Crane Prairie Dam, the waters of five other rivers and creeks have been added to it. There is no longer any confusion about whether it is a creek or a river. Broad and deep, it tumbles down a series of steep drops, then passes under the bridge on road 42. The bridge is the dividing point: upstream the river is steep and not fishable;

CRANE PRAIRIE

downstream it is quiet and offers excellent fishing.

Anglers can reach this three-mile stretch of river from the bridge at road 42 or by parking near the Sheep Springs campground. Trails follow the river, and it is wadeable in most places. The gradient is gradual, the river slow and meandering. Unlike the stretch between Crane Prairie and Little Lava, this part of the Deschutes passes through grasslands, but the trees have been logged.

It is late summer when this part of the Deschutes comes into its own. Big brown trout move up from Wickiup Reservoir preparatory to fall spawning. They can be caught on flies, and big streamers are the best tactic. Enjoy the fishing while you can: it's over at the end of August since this section has the same season as the stretch above Crane Prairie—June 1 through August 31.

An angler heads for a favorite spot on a foggy morning.

Bob Jones prepares to release a fly-caught brown trout at Wickiup Reservoir.

Wickiup Reservoir

For centuries, Indians hunted and fished at the site of Wickiup Reservoir. Their temporary shelters, called "wickiups," gave the area its name. In 1947 a dam was completed across the Deschutes River, and the area was flooded. At full pool, Wickiup Reservoir covers 15 square miles and is one of the largest bodies of water in Oregon. Wickiup doesn't remain at full pool for very long, though. Throughout the summer and fall, water flows out through irrigation pipes, and by the end of the fishing season the lake will have shrunk back to reveal wide expanses of grass and mud and many stumps. Drawn-down reservoirs are not a pretty sight and Wickiup is no exception.

All those ugly stumps, however, make good fish habitat when the water covers them. Unlike Crane Prairie, the Wickiup area was logged before it was flooded. Although it was not the original intent, the big root wads provided hiding places for brown trout, a fish that loves overhead cover. In addition, the woody debris was home to smaller fish and aquatic insects. Fifty years later, much of the wood has decayed, and the Oregon Department of Fish and Wildlife and the U.S. Forest Service have had a joint project to dump bundles of logs into the lake to improve the habitat. (Unfortunately the project often is postponed due to funding problems for both agencies.)

With the exception of the north end of the reservoir (near Sheep Springs) fly fishers stay away from Wickiup in droves. In fact, the times I've fished the main body of the lake, my companions and I have been the only ones fly fishing. There's no reason for this, however. I remember clearly the evening in early May that Bob Jones and I launched our float tubes and kicked around for a couple of hours. Near dusk, I looked over at Bob and saw his 8-weight Sage bent in a throbbing semi-circle. By the time I arrived to take a photo, he had an eight-pound brown trout in the net. Half an hour later, he yelled again. He had an even bigger fish on the line! To top it, the next morning he landed another brown, but this one was smaller—a mere five- or six-pounder.

Wickiup's fly fishing isn't always like that. Any time you make trophy brown trout your goal, you have to recognize you're going to get skunked more than a few times. But the fish are there, and they can be taken on flies.

The best rig for early season browns is a stout rod (at least a six-weight, and preferably an eight-weight) and a deep-sinking line. I prefer a full-sinking Wet Cel Type IV. Do you need a line that sinks that fast? When Bob Jones was catching his big browns I went fishless, and the only difference in our rigs was that he used a Type IV and I used a Type III. That little bit of extra depth—and the ability to *stay* at that depth—made the difference.

Flies for these fish should be big; Matukas, big leeches, wool-head sculpins, etc. The browns aren't real fussy, but they do need to see something big and lifelike.

Wickiup's brown trout can be found anywhere, but places where the wind or current gather baitfish are most likely, especially if there are places for the browns to hide. The face of the dam in spring, the water near Goose Island, and the deep water near the Deschutes channel are good places to look.

Brown trout spawn in the Deschutes above Wickiup Reservoir, so the water is closed to angling in the fall.

In July and August, shade is where you make it!

Wind can be a major problem for Wickiup anglers. The prevailing westerlies blow unimpeded across the lake, and they can pile up some big waves on the east shore. Anglers need to exercise caution and know when to leave the lake so they can fish another day.

As summer ends, the brown trout head to the north end of the lake. They will spawn in Browns Creek and the Deschutes above the reservoir. If you take a boat up the Deschutes arm in late August or September, you can often see huge browns cruising the deeper water like submarines on patrol. Fortunately, the Deschutes above Wickiup and all the lake north of Gull Point are closed to fishing after August 31.

In fall 1989, poachers from a community of Russian immigrants strung gillnets across Browns Creek, the major spawning tributary. When they were caught, they had over 150 dead brown trout, many well over ten pounds. This was their third or fourth "fishing" expedition that month, so the catch was light. One can only imagine how many big spawners were wiped out. The poachers' defense was that they thought the fish were carp, and they were let off with a slap on the wrist.

It is a tribute to Wickiup's productivity that the fishery has recovered, and brown trout are plentiful again—if not easy to catch.

Brown trout aren't Wickiup's only quarry for fly anglers. Landlocked coho salmon can provide excellent sport on fly tackle. Streamers (silver body, green wing) and bright patterns make the best flies. A few rainbows and brook trout are also available, and the Fish and Wildlife people tell me Wickiup has trophy whitefish. What brings most non-fly anglers to Wickiup is kokanee (landlocked sockeye salmon), but these cannot be reliably taken on flies.

Wickiup has many campgrounds, most of which are only useful in spring. As the lake is drained for irrigation, all campgrounds are left far from the water except those at the north end. The reliable all-season campsites are at Gull Point, West South Twin, and Sheep Springs. The former two are full-service campgrounds, while the latter is rougher and has only limited facilities.

Twin Lakes Resort operates a full-hookup RV park near Gull Point. The resort also rents cabins and boats, and has a restaurant.

Birds And Wildlife

Fish aren't the only wild animals at Crane Prairie. The lake abounds in wildlife, especially waterfowl. Osprey, eagles, cormorants, ducks, geese, cranes, and many others call Crane

Prairie home for much of the year, and anglers are often distracted from their fishing by the never-ending show staged by the local birds. I never venture onto this lake without binoculars. Sometimes I use them to spot fish or see what other anglers are up to, but usually they are used to observe birds.

Bird-watching anglers need to give wild critters their space, however, especially during breeding season. Don't tie your boat to a snag that has a nest in it, and if a nesting bird is yelling at you, move away. In its fuss, a bird may crush its eggs or kick youngsters out of the nest.

Following are some of the critters you can expect to see at Crane Prairie.

Osprey

Crane Prairie is the largest osprey nesting site in Oregon. There is rarely a time when the high-pitched chirping of these birds cannot be heard. And more than one angler has been unnerved by the splash the big raptors make when they smack the water in search of fish.

Osprey belong to the hawk family. The majority of their prey is fish, but they will also eat amphibians, snakes, and rodents. Osprey nests are big and located in the tops of snags near the shore. Early in the season, look at the nests through binoculars and you'll probably see young osprey—all beak and fluff—peering over the edge.

I'd love to fish like an osprey. They soar high over the lake looking for their quarry, then when they spot a fish near the surface, they hover briefly, fold their wings back, and plummet like a rock, hitting the water head first. Usually they come up with a trout or a bass in their talons and fly off to a snag to eat it. Once an osprey nails its prey and flies off, it turns the fish so its head will face forward and be more aerodynamic. By the

An osprey dines on a luckless trout.

Crane Prairie

Crane Prairie is home to a variety of waterfowl.

way, osprey don't fish with barbless hooks: their talons have small barbules to help hold their slippery catch.

Oregon's osprey migrate to Central and South America for the winter; most have left Crane Prairie by mid-September. They return in March or early April.

Bald Eagles

While not as common as osprey, bald eagles are often seen at Crane Prairie. They feed on fish, carrion, rodents, and even an occasional duck.

The eagles begin to nest when they are three to five years old. If you're lucky, you'll see the courtship ritual of two eagles: the male and female lock talons in mid-air, then fall to earth, separating at the last possible moment.

Unlike osprey, bald eagles stay in the area through the winter. In fact, resident birds are joined by migrants from outside the state, and there are more birds in winter than in summer.

Great Blue Herons

Stately great blue herons reside at Crane Prairie and feed on small fish and amphibians. They'll also eat mice. All human anglers would benefit from studying a heron's fishing tactics. They pick a good spot, then stand still as a statue and wait for the right moment. When a fish or frog comes near, they strike quickly and precisely.

In winter, heron will follow open water. If Crane Prairie doesn't freeze over, they might stay at the lake. Otherwise, they will move east or west in search of ice-free water.

Sandhill Cranes

Crane Prairie does have cranes, but not many. Actually, the area was probably named for the herons rather than true cranes. Several pairs of sandhills will reside at the lake through the summer, and others make a short stop-over. Most anglers never see the big birds, but they often hear them. They have a loud, rattling call that sounds like someone trying to yodel and gargle at the same time. And they'll do it at night, too; I've been kept from a good night's sleep more than once by noisy cranes.

Bald eagles are a common sight at Crane Prairie.

Cormorants

Cormorants look like big, sleek ducks. They are fish-eaters, diving and swimming for their meals. The ones at Crane

Cormorants nest in Crane Prairie's standing snags. Give nesting birds lots of space.

Prairie are double-crested cormorants; they are native to Oregon. Cormorants love to congregate in snags overlooking good fishing grounds, and I sometimes expect them to hold up little numbers as they judge my casting skills.

Other Birds And Wildlife
Besides the birds mentioned above, Crane Prairie hosts a plethora of ducks, including merganser, mallard, widgeon, pintail, gadwall, and bufflehead. I've seen a raft of coots that stretched over a quarter mile (I'm talking about the duck, not old fly fishers in float tubes). Canada geese and red-tail hawks are also common, and both trumpeter and tundra swans make occasional appearances.

Shore animals include elk, mule and blacktail deer, cougar, black bear, and others. Don't worry about the cougar and bear, though. There is an even more terrifying mammal stalking you at Crane Prairie—a ferocious, aggressive, toothsome creature that would destroy you, your campsite, and your family if given half a chance. I'm talking about that dreaded beast, the Crane Prairie ground squirrel.

You might think these guys are chipmunks, cute little Chip and Dale types. No way. These are actually golden-mantled ground squirrels (no stripes on the head), and I've never encountered more bold and obnoxious rodents than those living at Crane Prairie.

Take these animals seriously. They are chipmunks with chutzpah, squirrels with an attitude. To deter these rodents, the nation needs an effective SDI (Squirrel Defense Initiative).

If you look away for ten seconds, they will be into your food, your cooler, your tent, your shorts. I've had them run right up my leg in an attempt to steal a bite from my sandwich. They've scampered across my chest when I've attempted a daytime nap; had I not wakened, they would have been in my beard nibbling bits of leftover yogurt. Nothing is safe from them: food, soap, paper towels; you name it, they eat it. Moral: put *everything* away, and don't turn your back. And don't try to take a nap on open ground.

The terror of Crane Prairie — the gold-mantled ground squirrel.

CRANE PRAIRIE

Summer sunsets can be spectacular.

Controversies

Crane Prairie is not without controversy. The lake has a large constituency of users whose interests are diverse and sometimes conflicting. Most of the controversy centers on the introduction of largemouth bass, regulations, and dragonfly harvesting.

Bass

Largemouth bass were illegally introduced to Crane Prairie sometime in the 1980s. They thrived in the rich waters, and the lake is now known for trophy largemouth as well as big trout. Bass boats are as common on the lake as float tubes. The bass seem to have "leaked" through the dam and are now in Wickiup reservoir, from whence they may be further distributed to the upper Deschutes River.

Originally it was believed that the trout and bass would happily co-exist in Crane Prairie because the lake's temperature variation would naturally segregate them. It was further believed that the bass would prey primarily on chub, a forage the trout left alone. Unfortunately it didn't work out that way.

While there is some segregation due to temperature, with more bass seeking warmer water at the south end of the lake and avoiding the cold inflows from the Deschutes, a lot of bass are found in areas that used to be the exclusive domain of trout. Further, the chub population was devastated by water drawdowns, so now bass and trout compete for the same food.

Some anglers—most of them fly fishers—feel the Oregon Department of Fish and Wildlife (ODFW) didn't do enough to eliminate bass from the lake when they were first introduced. They feel that ODFW rewarded those who illegally introduced the fish by allowing the largemouth to remain unchecked in the lake and keeping a catch limit on them. They point out that bass have now been illegally introduced into Davis Lake, a nearby fly-fishing-only stillwater that also grows big rainbows. Since it is nearly impossible to stop illegal fish transportation, and the perpetrators are allowed to achieve their goal, what reason do they have to cease their clandestine introductions?

The result of illegal stocking could be chaos: disease introductions, declining trout size due to food competition, etc. As one fly angler asked, "What's next for Crane Prairie? Pike and walleye?" A good question, made more chilling when you realize that bluegill are now showing up in the catch.

Regulations

A few years ago, Greg Price, a Bend-area fly-shop owner, suggested that Crane Prairie should have "trophy fish" regulations, and the limit should be reduced to one fish per angler per day. The proposal was later modified to a two-fish-per-day limit.

Soon after word of his proposal hit the streets, Greg felt like he'd been run over by a freight train. A weekly fishing and hunting tabloid that often features photos of big (and dead) Crane Prairie rainbows published letters and editorials castigating him. A local bait fishing guide jumped in, too. It was claimed that fly anglers wanted Crane's fish to themselves and were trying to drive bait fishermen off the lake.

"All I wanted was to save a few fish," Greg said.

The current bag limit is five trout per day, with only one fish over 20 inches. Unfortunately, the regulation is frequently violated. "There's little enforcement on the lake," says Fred Foisset, a fly-fishing guide who works Crane Prairie and other local stillwaters. "Last week I saw a guy in a canoe kill five big fish, all well over 20 inches. He pulled out at a remote spur road. How do you stop people like that?" By the way, the poacher was a fly angler.

Another problem is artificial bait, the most common of which is Power Bait from Berkeley Tackle. Power Bait is very popular with bait anglers, especially beginners, and is an awesome fish attractant. I've experimented with the stuff on put-

Gut-hooked on bait, then released, a trout struggles in vain against its death.

CRANE PRAIRIE

and-take waters, and believe me, trout inhale it. Every fish had the hook embedded far down its throat.

Recent scientific studies confirm this. They show that 80% of all fish hooked on artificial bait are critically hooked, either gut-hooked or hooked in the gill arches. Further, the studies show that half of these fish will die. Mortality is especially high if the hook is removed, as is usually the case. In contrast, the mortality rate for fly-caught trout is around 4%—even lower if the angler is skilled at handling fish. So anglers who catch and release big trout that they hooked on artificial bait are kidding themselves.

Furthermore, many trout hooked on artificial bait break off. They still have a hook in their gut, and studies show that around 30% of them die within a few weeks. Perhaps the old adage should be changed to "the big one that got away—and went belly up the next week."

When it comes to trout harvesting, the irony is that Crane Prairie's big fish are terrible table fare. From June through mid-September—the period of heaviest fishing pressure—there's no point in keeping any fish; they taste like a stew made from mud and algae. As one angler says, "They taste like the lake smells." It's disheartening to think how many trophy trout are taken home, proudly shown to the neighbors, then tossed into the garbage can.

Dragonfly Harvest

Dragonfly nymphs are a popular bait on Crane Prairie. The good news is that trout caught on the nymphs by a skilled and attentive angler are usually lip-hooked and can be released (or break off) with little damage to the fish. The bad news is that there is a lot of dragonfly nymph harvesting going on. Some of it is done by anglers who will use the bait themselves, but some of it is done by commercial harvesters who sell the bait to stores who resell to anglers at prices that sometimes reach $5 or more per dozen.

Although Crane Prairie is large enough that it would seem difficult to strip its dragonfly population, other lakes are not. Commercial harvesters regularly visit small lakes in the area and pick out every nymph they can find. Many of these lakes have limited dragonfly habitat in concentrated, easily reached areas. It doesn't take much effort to reduce their dragonfly population below recoverable levels. Furthermore, much of this harvesting is happening in the national forest, and a permit is required for any commercial venture on federal land. No permits have ever been issued to nymph harvesters.

Everyone agrees that the size of Crane Prairie's trout has dropped so that it is rare to see a fish over seven pounds anymore. Is it because the dragonfly population is greatly reduced?

A bait fisherman searches for dragonfly numphs to use for bait. Activities such as this, combined with predation by illegally-introduced bass, have devastated Crane Prairie's once-abundant dragonfly population.

A proud angler displays her catch.

A Personal View

Even if you proved that a trophy catch-and-release fishery on Crane Prairie would improve the resource, cost the state less money, and bring more dollars into the local economy than the current regulations, it probably wouldn't happen. Unfortunately, politics plays as large a role in fisheries regulations as science and economics. Crane Prairie has a large constituency of local bait anglers, and anyone who suggests outlawing bait in general and Power Bait in particular, or that the bag limit be reduced, will be pilloried. And any fisheries manager who suggests it will suffer even worse pressure. Politically, it's just not going to happen anytime soon.

Frankly, I don't have a problem with people fishing with bait. My only complaint is with those who abuse the resource, and no fishing method is free of abusive users.

Resource abusers fall into two groups: those who don't know any better, and those who don't care. The former can be reached through education. The latter are controlled with regulation and, most importantly, enforcement.

Therefore, I would like to see posters put up around Crane Prairie that told people that the fish don't taste good in the summer months, and that explained proper catch-and-release methods—including the fact that artificial bait kills a lot of fish. This would educate at least some of the people who don't know any better. It would also create peer pressure on other anglers to treat the resource with more care.

While I doubt that a season-long reduction in the bag limit is politically viable, I think there is another option. Late in the season, Crane Prairie's trout often concentrate in the channels and feed heavily. From mid-September to the end of the season (October 31), fish fatten up for winter and are often easy to catch. If these fish were not killed, more natural spawners would head up the creeks to create the trophies of the future. Doesn't it make more sense to have these fish on the spawning redds rather than on the dinner plate? Increased natural reproduction would save a cash-strapped agency the cost of stocking trout. Therefore, I'd like to see a no-kill regulation from September 15 to October 31.

I would also like to see the bag limit on bass removed. I don't have a problem with bass; they're a great fish and good sport on flies. But I do have a problem when we reward people who play Russian roulette with our fisheries by illegally moving fish from one water to another.

I also feel that commercial harvesting of dragonfly nymphs should be ended. Too much of this happens in fragile ecosystems.

Finally, no regulations are effective if they are not enforced. I realize that the state police are stretched thin, but a few simple creel checks would improve compliance. The key is to be sneaky about it. Setting up a checkpoint at one boat ramp will do little to deter serious violators. However, if the police were undercover and on the water, they would be more likely to catch poachers. If they did this once a week for a few weeks, they'd have the poachers so paranoid they'd spend more time looking over their shoulder than killing fish.

Canoes can be used on Crane Prairie, but watch the wind — the lake can get rough quickly.

Regulations

Always check the synopsis of Oregon angling regulations for the final word, and watch for notices posted near the lake. Sometimes there are special closures or regulations that are in effect for a limited time or suddenly enacted.

Season

Open from the fourth Saturday in April through October 31. All Crane Prairie tributaries are closed after August 31, and many do not open until June 1; check the angling synopsis for any tributary you intend to fish.

Trout Limits

Up to five trout per day may be kept, with a six-inch minimum. Only one trout over 20 inches may be kept.

Bass Limits

Up to five bass per day may be kept, with no more than three over 15 inches.

Hours

Closed to angling from one hour after sunset to one hour before sunrise. This applies to all species of fish, including bass.

Boating

There is a 10 mph speed limit.

Accommodations And Services

Campgrounds

There are over 70 campgrounds within 30 miles of Crane Prairie. Those closest to the lake are listed below. For a complete description of all the campgrounds in the Cascade Lakes area, see my book *Fishing in Oregon's Cascade Lakes*.

All the campgrounds listed here are Forest Service facilities, but they are managed by private contractors. Unless stated otherwise, each campsite has a picnic table, fire pit, and parking spot, and each campground has trash receptacles, drinking water, and pit toilets (outhouses).

Crane Prairie sits in a lodgepole pine forest. These are skinny trees with narrow crowns, which guarantees that there will be little shade at high noon, regardless of which campsite you pick.

Most campgrounds are suitable for RVs of reasonable size, but none have hook-ups. See the section below for private RV parks in the area.

Crane Prairie Resort has a few supplies, flies, and boat rentals.

Crane Prairie

Crane Prairie has several excellent campgrounds.

CAMPGROUNDS

Crane Prairie

This campground is so big it has maps so you won't get lost. There are 146 sites along paved roads. Some sites are designed for use by multiple family groups and have extra parking and tables; however, use is restricted to two or more families (these sites are clearly marked). Four campsites are barrier-free for the handicapped. Sites 91-96 are tent-only sites. There are two boat ramps. The resort is nearby. $10 per night.

Rock Creek

There are 32 sites here. Nine are along a dirt road near the lake, and 23 are on paved cul-de-sacs. There is a boat ramp. Because this campground (and the one nearby at Quinn River) backs up on road 46, traffic noise in summer can be unpleasant to those not used to it. I'm just a country boy, so June through August I go somewhere else. $9 per night.

Quinn River. Forty-one campsites are distributed along a dirt road. This campground offers more privacy than Rock Creek, but it suffers from summer traffic noise (see Rock Creek). There's a boat ramp. $9 per night.

Continued on page 44

Cow Meadow

This rough campground has 19 campsites, but there is no drinking water. They say there is a boat ramp, but don't believe it. $5 per night.

Mile Camp

This primitive facility is north of Crane Prairie near the Deschutes River. It is just off road 46. Other than two outhouses, there are few facilities here: no water, no garbage pickup, no tables. It is a singularly dusty and unattractive campground, but it is free.

Little Lava Lake

This is another primitive site, but better than Mile Camp. There are outhouses and garbage pickup, but no water or designated sites. The campground is at Little Lava Lake and borders the Deschutes River where it issues from the lake. $5 per night.

Lava Lake

Forty-four sites are scattered among the trees and have the usual amenities. The resort is nearby. $9 per night.

RV PARKS AND RESORTS

Three resorts in the area offer full hook-up RV facilities: Crane Prairie, Lava Lake, and Twin Lakes. See the section above for more information. Phone numbers for reservations are:

Crane Prairie: 541/383-3939
Lava Lake: 541/382-9443
Twin Lakes: 541/593-6526

Bend

Bend is the biggest town in Central Oregon and has every service an angler could want. The Central Oregon Chamber of Commerce will provide potential visitors with free guide books on lodging, dining, and other services in the area. They can be reached at 541/382-3221, or write or visit their office at 63085 N. Highway 97, Bend, OR 97701

Sunriver

This is a luxury resort with multiple golf courses, swimming pools, an airport, shopping malls, tennis courts, and other amenities you never knew you needed. There are extensive overnight accommodations, including condominiums and houses to rent. The phone number for the main lodge is 541/593-1221.

Big trout, mountain scenery . . . Does it get any better?

CRANE PRAIRIE

RESORTS

The resorts in this area are simple facilities with a few conveniences for campers and anglers. Only two—Twin Lakes and Cultus Lake—have overnight accommodations and a restaurant.

Crane Prairie services include:
RV park with 31 full-hookup spaces
Store with sundries, limited groceries, tackle and flies
Boat and motor rental
Guide service
Showers and Laundromat
Gas and propane
Emergency phone

Cultus Lake services include:
18 cabins with kitchens, 5 without
Restaurant
Store with sundries, limited groceries, tackle and flies
Gas and propane
Emergency phone

Lava Lake services include:
RV park with 24 full-hookup spaces
Store with sundries, limited groceries, tackle and flies
Showers and Laundromat
Holding tank dump station
Gas and propane
Emergency phone

Twin Lakes services include:
RV park with full hook-ups
Seven log cabins plus two studio four-plexes, all with kitchens
Restaurant
Store with sundries, limited groceries, tackle and flies
Boat and motor rental for Wickiup Reservoir
Gas and propane
Showers and Laundromat
Emergency phone

FLY SHOPS

You know the fishing's good when there are so many fly shops around. They include:

Deschutes Fly and Tackle
15746 Burgess Rd., La Pine. 541/536-1441.

Deschutes River Outfitters
61115 S. Highway 97, Bend. 541/388-8191.

Deschutes River Outfitters, Sunriver
Sunriver Lodge, Sunriver. 541/593-1221, X4100.

Dexter's Fly Shop
52582 Highway 97, La Pine. 541/536-9038.

Hook Wine and Cheddar/Cascade Guides and Outfitters
Building 22, Sunriver Village Mall (PO Box 4548) Sunriver. 541/593-1633 or 541/593-2358.

Sunriver Outfitters
#1 Venture Lane, Sunriver Business Park (PO Box 3012) Sunriver. 541/593-8814.

The Fly Box
1293 NE 3rd (Highway 97), Bend. 541/388-3330.

The Patient Angler
55 NW Wall St., Bend. 541/389-6208.

Guides
You can obtain the names and phone numbers for guides who specialize in fly fishing this area by calling any of the fly shops previously listed.

Forest Service
The fishing area described in this book is part of the Deschutes National Forest. The U.S. Forest Service office in Bend has responsibility for the roads and facilities. Call them at 541/388-5664 to check road conditions, etc.

Oregon Department of Fish and Wildlife
Weekly fishing reports for Oregon's Central region can be heard by dialing 800/275-3474 (800-ASK-FISH). ODFW also has a home page on the Internet with a weekly fishing report. The address is http://www.dfw.state.or.us/

Crane Prairie

Treat yourself
and your angling partner...

...to a fly fishing and tying feast with subscriptions to *Flyfishing & Tying Journal.* You'll marvel at the helpful, colorful creativity inside this 100-plus page quarterly masterpiece of publishing!

You've worked hard, now sit back and drink in the elixir of fly-fishing potential that we provide you, featuring fine printing on top-quality paper. We are terribly excited with our generous, friendly fly-fishing publication and know you will love it also! Please share our joy of discovery and subscribe today!

Strike a deal for only $15.00 for one year.

Order a subscription below for you and your angling friend.

TO SUBSCRIBE
CALL
1-800-541-9498

(9-5 Monday thru Friday, Pacific Time)

Or Use The Coupon Below

SUBSCRIBE/ORDER HERE!

Please send me:
- ☐ One year of *Flyfishing & Tying Journal* for only $15.00 (4 big issues)
- ☐ Two years of *Flyfishing & Tying Journal* for only $25.00 (8 issues)
- ☐ Check enclosed (US Funds) ☐ New ☐ Renew
- ☐ Charge to:
- ☐ Visa ☐ MC CC#:_____ Exp: _____

(Canadian & foreign orders please add $5/year)

Phone orders: 1-800-541-9498 or 503-653-8108. FAX 503-653-2766. Call 8 to 5 M-F, Pacific Standard Time.

Name:_____   Name:_____

Day Phone:(____) _____   Day Phone:(____) _____

Address:_____   Address:_____

_____   _____

City:_____ State:___ Zip:____   City:_____ State:___ Zip:____

FRANK AMATO PUBLICATIONS • P.O. BOX 82112 • PORTLAND, OR 97282